First published in 2024 by Publisher

© Natasha Harris 2024

The moral rights of the author have been asserted
All rights reserved. Except as permitted under the Australian Copyright Act 1968 (for example, a fair dealing for the purposes of study, research, criticism or review), no part of this book may be reproduced, stored in a retrieval system, communicated or transmitted in any form or by any means without prior written permission.

All inquiries should be made to the author.

A dedication to my little inspirations, Bella, Violette & co.

I AM...

Affirmation statements for children

Written by Natasha Leevi Harris
Illustrated by Afsaneh Bagherloo

I am Bella, and I am
BRAVE.

I am Scarlett, and I am
STRONG.

I use my imagination to create beautiful art!

I am Evie, and I am ENOUGH.

May I always remember this on days that are rough.

One day, I will achieve something brilliant!

I show this to others by sharing.

I am Violette, and I am PERFECTLY MADE.

A rare individual who shines even in the shade.

I try my best to include people and not ever be neglectful.

I am Ryder, and I am UNIQUE.

There's nothing that you can't do when you believe in . . .

www.ingramcontent.com/pod-product-compliance
Lightning Source LLC
Chambersburg PA
CBRC101937290426
44109CB00010B/181